20 WAYS TO COOK
SOUP

*Geoff and Lin Chapman own a success-
ful, highly-rated restaurant,* **Le Petit
Canard**, *in rural West Dorset.
Originally from Canada, they have
worked in several countries and de-
scribe their cooking as modern French
with oriental overtones.*

20 Ways to Cook
SOUP

Geoff and Lin Chapman

Thomas Harmsworth Publishing Company

Acknowledgement
Grateful thanks to Peter Woodger of M.W.
Antiques for providing the premises and
the props for the photography.

First Published 1994 by
Thomas Harmsworth Publishing
Company
Old Rectory Offices
Stoke Abbott, Beaminster
Dorset DT8 3JT, United Kingdom

British Library Cataloguing-in-Publication
Data. A catalogue record for this book is
available from the British Library.

ISSN 1355-4050
ISBN 0 948807 21 0

Printed and bound in Great Britain by
BPC Paulton Books Limited

CONTENTS

INTRODUCTION

In many countries soup is the main daily meal. Usually concocted without a recipe, just with skill and imagination from whatever happens to be fresh and abundant at the time — be it market produce, home-grown vegetables or even yesterday's leftovers.

Soup is certainly, in its simple, less sophisticated form, pure comfort food. Warming and hearty, restorative and easily digested.

The term is believed to have originated from the word 'sop', which is the bread over which the broth was poured — and bread has always been such an integral part of a soup course, either as a crusty loaf to accompany, or as croûtons, or even simple torn bread pieces in the liquid itself.

Sadly today, the convenience of ready-made foods has led people away from this most simple and delicious home-made food that takes so little time and effort to prepare. Consider the amazing versatility of a dish that can be adapted to virtually any ingredient: vegetables, poultry, meat, fish, fruit, which can result in a soup of silky or chunky texture that may be served hot or cold in rustic or highly refined style. What a dish!

GETTING DOWN TO BASICS

The basis of a good soup is generally:

a) strongly flavoured ingredients such as onion, tomato, garlic, that easily give up their flavour to a liquid for a simply prepared one-stage soup.

 or

b) a well-flavoured, pre-prepared stock which is used as a base liquid to enhance the flavour and texture of other ingredients. For example, a beef and vegetable soup would be created from the flavours of the meat juices and the stronger vegetables, whereas a mushroom soup would benefit greatly from the depth of flavour a little stock would add, be it poultry or vegetable-based stock.

STOCKS

Stocks are often thought of as the domain of the professional chef, so home cooks might be pleasantly surprised to learn just how simple stock preparation actually is.

All stocks follow the same basic principles. Raw ingredients: fish, meat, poultry and/or vegetables, are simmered in water until the liquid becomes infused with the flavours. The flavoured liquid is strained and skimmed and becomes the foundation of soups or sauces.

It is advisable to make a large amount (use the biggest pot in the house) and divide up the remaining stock into smaller containers for freezing. This allows you to whip up delicious and nutritious soups at short notice with virtually no work involved. Reckon on 8 fl oz (225 ml) per person for soup.

COOKING TERMS

Sauté: gentle, shallow-fry in butter or oil, or a mixture of the two.

Purée: ingredients blended to a fine, smooth consistency. This can be achieved with either a hand blender, food processor or manually with a food mill.

Simmering: very gentle boiling.

Julienne: cut into the size and shape of matchsticks.

EQUIPMENT

Soup Pot: A heavy-bottomed pot large enough to allow for the ingredients, plus room for the liquid to expand and boil.

Hand Blender: Handy piece of equipment (electric) that allows puréeing in the soup pot. Available from all major appliance stores.

INGREDIENTS

In all the recipes where cream is mentioned, you can use single cream, double cream, whipping cream or crème fraîche.

Several soups offer the option of stock or water. While water is acceptable, expect less flavour and body in the finished soup.

Cheese Croûtons

Cut small cubes from day-old bread and toss in bowl with a little melted butter or olive oil. Add finely-grated parmesan (to taste) and toss well.

 3

Bake on sheet in medium oven until golden. May be stored in airtight container for 2 - 3 days.

Herb Croûtons
Make as for cheese croûtons; omit cheese and substitute a sprinkling of mixed, dried herbs and a little sea salt (to taste).

FISH STOCK

Makes: approximately 7½ pints (4.25 litres) stock
Preparation time: 15 minutes
Cooking time: 45 minutes

5 lbs (2.25 kg) fish bones
4 celery sticks, chopped coarsely
2 onions, peeled and chopped coarsely
1 small leek, washed and chopped
2 carrots, peeled and chopped coarsely
8 pints (4.54 litres) of water
2 bay leaves
1 teaspoon thyme
3 sprigs parsley
1 teaspoon tarragon

Put all the vegetables and herbs in the biggest pot in the house with 1 pint (550 ml) of water. Cover and sweat the mixture over low heat for 15 minutes. Do not brown the vegetables.

Meanwhile, rinse the fish bones under cold, running water a couple of times.

Add the fish bones and the remainder of the water to the pot.

 4

Bring to the boil and then simmer for 30 minutes.

Remove from the heat and strain the stock.

Cool and refrigerate the stock until required.

You may make a fish velouté as soon as the stock is strained. You will find it easier to do when the stock is already hot.

Chef's tips:
☆ Do not simmer the stock for much longer than the 30 minutes or the liquid will become cloudy and/or bitter.
☆ Sole or turbot bones are ideal for a tasty stock.

FISH VELOUTÉ

2 oz (50 gm) butter
4 tablespoons flour
32 fl oz (900 ml) fish stock

Melt the butter in a heavy saucepan, add the flour and cook, stirring continually over medium heat for 3 minutes.

Whisk in the stock, bring to a simmer for 10 minutes and skim off the scum that will form on top. Simmer a further 5 minutes and then strain.

CHICKEN STOCK

Makes: about 8 pints (4.5 litres) of chicken stock
Preparation time: 15 minutes
Cooking time: 2 hours

5 lbs (2.25 kg) of chicken bones, backs, wings, feet & necks
1 large onion, peeled and chopped coarsely
2 carrots, peeled and chopped
3 celery sticks, washed and chopped
1 leek, washed and chopped coarsely
10 pints (5.6 litres) of water
3 bay leaves
½ tablespoon thyme
½ bulb of garlic
4 big sprigs of parsley

Put all the ingredients into the biggest pot avail-

 6

able and bring to a boil.

Simmer uncovered for 2 - 3 hours.

Strain the stock and cool quickly. Refrigerate, covered, until needed.

Before you use the stock, lift off and discard the solid fat layer.

Chef's tips:
☆ The longer you allow the stock to reduce the stronger and deeper the flavour.

If you have a pot big enough, make the quantity above. If not, scale the recipe down accordingly. Once made, the stock can be frozen in smaller containers. Allow for 8 fl oz (225 ml) per person for soup when dividing up the stock.

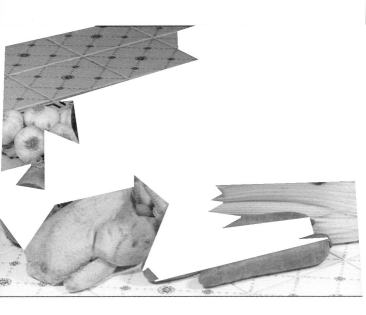

CHICKEN VELOUTÉ

2 oz (50 gm) butter
4 tablespoons flour
32 fl oz (900 ml) chicken stock

Melt the butter in a heavy saucepan, stir in the flour and cook, stirring continually over medium heat for 3 minutes.

Whisk in the stock, bring to a simmer for 10 minutes and skim off the scum that will form on the top. Simmer a further 5 minutes and then strain.

Fish and chicken stocks can be the building blocks for most soups, and can be used as soups with the addition of seasoning to taste.

IMPERIAL/METRIC CONVERSIONS

Dry weight		Liquid measure	
ounces	grams	fluid ounces	millilitres
1	25	1	25
2	50	2	50
3	75	3	75-90
4 (¼ lb)	125	4	125
5	150	5 (¼ pint)	150
6	175	6	175
7	200	7	200
8 (½ lb)	225	8	225
9	250	9	250
10	275	10 (½ pint)	275
11	300	11	300
12 (¾ lb)	350	12	350
13	375	13	375
14	400	14	400
15	425	15 (¾ pint)	425
16 (1 lb)	450	16	450
17	475	17	475
18	500	18	500
2¼ lb	1000 (1 kilo)	20 (1 pint)	550
		1¾ pints	1000 (1 litre)

WATERCRESS SOUP

Serves: 4
Preparation time: 10 minutes
Cooking time: 35 minutes
Suitable for dinner party: Yes
Suitable first course: Yes
Suitable microwave cooking: No
Suitable freezing: Yes
Special equipment: Hand blender or food processor
Calorie content: Medium-low
Carbohydrate content: High
Fibre content: High
Protein content: Medium-high
Fat content: Medium-low

This is a great all-year, any-occasion soup. Simple and quick to prepare, inexpensive and just chock full of valuable nutrients. (Vitamins A and D, Calcium, Iron, Iodine; and just 2 oz of watercress contains the body's total recommended daily allowance of Vitamin C!)

 10

12 oz (3 bunches) (350 gm) watercress		
10 oz (275 gm) leeks, washed and coarsely chopped		
1 small onion, peeled and coarsely chopped		
8 - 10 oz (225 - 275 gm) potatoes, peeled, coarsely cut		
30 fl oz (850 ml) chicken stock, water (or mixture of both)		
2 oz (50 gm) butter		
2 fl oz (50 ml) cream		
seasoning		

Melt the butter in a large saucepan. Add the leeks and onions and sauté gently, without browning, for 8 - 10 minutes.

Add the chicken stock (or water) and the potatoes and bring to a boil. Lower heat and simmer for 15 to 20 minutes until the potatoes are soft.

Remove from the stove and add in the washed watercress. Stir, cover and leave to rest for one minute whilst the watercress wilts.

Purée the mixture and return to heat. Bring the soup to a simmer, stir in the cream and season to taste.

Chef's tip:
☆ Single cream or crème fraîche can replace the double cream.

Wine:
☆ A light, fresh, fruity Red — perhaps Beaujolais, young Loire Red or Chianti. Alternatively a big flavour White, for example crisp, bold-style Chardonnay or a Tokay-Pinot Gris from Alsace.

CRAB AND MUSHROOM BISQUE

Serves: 4
Preparation time: 10 - 15 minutes
Cooking time: 25 minutes
Suitable for dinner party: Yes
Suitable first course: Yes
Suitable microwave cooking: No
Suitable freezing: Yes
Special equipment: None
Calorie content: Moderate
Carbohydrate content: Low
Fibre content: Quite low
Protein content: Medium
Fat content: Quite low

A delicious and sophisticated bisque to delight your dinner guests. If you are unable to find brown crab meat ask your local fishmonger if he can order vac-packed or frozen crab meat from his supplier.

 13

10 oz (275 gm) brown crab meat
12 oz (350 gm) mushrooms, sliced
1 medium onion in small dice
2 cloves of garlic, crushed
32 fl oz (900 ml) velouté (see page 6) - from fish stock or water
1 tablespoon tomato paste
2 teaspoons tarragon
2 oz (50 gm) butter

Sauté the mushrooms, onion and garlic in the butter for 5 - 7 minutes over low heat, without browning.

Add the tomato paste, increase the heat slightly and continue stirring for a further 2 minutes.

Pour in the velouté, add the tarragon and crab meat, stirring well to incorporate all the ingredients.

Bring to the boil and simmer gently for 10 minutes, stirring occasionally.

Season to taste with sea-salt and freshly ground pepper.

Serving suggestion:
☆ For a really special soup, garnish with shelled baby shrimp and clipped chives.

Wine:
☆ Any big character white with a bit of fruit would be good, e.g. a buttery, rich Chardonnay or perhaps a Pinot Gris or an Australian Riesling.

CARROT, GINGER AND HONEY SOUP

Serves: 4
Preparation time: 10 minutes
Cooking time: 40 minutes
Suitable for dinner party: Yes
Suitable first course: Yes
Suitable microwave cooking: Reheating only
Suitable freezing: Yes
Special equipment: Hand blender or food processor
Calorie content: Quite low
Carbohydrate content: Medium - high
Fibre content: Medium - high
Protein content: Low
Fat content: Low (without cream)

Carrots and honey have a marvellous affinity, and a touch of ginger adds an interesting twist to this classic combination. This is a simply-made and inexpensive soup that is a delicious and sophisticated way to start a meal.

 16

2 lbs (900 gm) carrots, peeled and coarsely cut
1 medium onion, peeled and coarsely cut
1½ oz (37.5 gm) fresh ginger, peeled and chopped fine
36 fl oz (1 litre) water
2 bay leaves
3 to 4 cloves garlic, peeled and whole
2 tablespoon runny honey
2 fl oz (50 ml) double cream or crème fraîche (optional)
1½ oz (37.5 gm) butter
seasoning

 17

Melt the butter in a large saucepan and add the carrots, onion, ginger, bay leaves and the garlic. Sauté gently, whilst stirring, for 5 minutes.

Add the water and bring to the boil then turn down the heat and let the mixture simmer for 30 minutes.

Remove the bay leaves and blend the liquid and solids to a fine purée.

Strain the purée through a sieve, pressing with a ladle to extract all the juices.

Return to the stove and add the honey and cream. Then slowly bring to the boil, stirring constantly.

Season to taste and serve.

Chef's tip:
☆ The ginger can be omitted and replaced by 2 teaspoons of fresh, chopped dill.

Wine:
☆ Try a chilled glass of Fino sherry with this intricately flavoured soup.

 18

SUNDAY ROAST SOUP

Serves: 4
Preparation time: 15 minutes
Cooking time: 40 minutes
Suitable for dinner party: No
Suitable first course: Better as a one-course lunch
   or light meal
Suitable microwave cooking: Reheating only
Suitable freezing: Yes
Special equipment: None
Calorie content: Medium
Carbohydrate content: Medium
Fibre content: Medium
Protein content: Medium
Fat content: Medium

 19

1½ oz (37.5 gm) butter
4 oz (125 gm) leeks, washed and sliced
2 carrots, peeled and diced quite small
1 medium potato, peeled and diced
pinch of rosemary
2 bay leaves
1 teaspoon dried thyme
1 teaspoon dried tarragon
1 small onion, peeled and diced
4 garlic cloves, peeled and crushed
40 fl oz (1.1 litres) water
8 - 10 oz (225 - 275 gm) lamb, beef or pork, diced
seasoning

Melt the butter in a large saucepan.

Add the carrots, onion, garlic, herbs, leek and bay leaves. Stir for 10 minutes over medium heat.

Add the water, meat and the potatoes, then bring to the boil and simmer for 30 minutes, stirring occasionally.

Season with salt and pepper to taste and serve.

Serving suggestion:
☆ This soup makes a hearty one course meal served with lots of crusty bread.

Chef's tip:
☆ The flavours of this soup will improve overnight and it can be stored for several days, but

be sure to boil for at least 5 minutes before
serving.

Wine:
☆ A medium bodied Red would be ideal here,
perhaps a youngish Bordeaux or Australian
Shiraz.

MUSHROOM SOUP

Serves: 4
Preparation time: 15 minutes
Cooking time: 25 minutes
Suitable for dinner party: Yes
Suitable first course: Yes
Suitable microwave cooking: Reheating only
Suitable freezing: Yes
Special equipment: None
Calorie content: Quite low
Carbohydrate content: Medium
Fibre content: Medium-high
Protein content: Low
Fat content: Quite low

If you like mushrooms — and most people seem to — you will adore this rich, earthy soup. Enjoy it for lunch with plenty of crusty bread or as an elegant and delicious first course at dinner.

 22

1 lb (450 gm) mushrooms, sliced
1½ oz (37.5 gm) butter
1 small onion, cut into small dice
2 to 3 cloves of garlic, peeled and crushed
1 teaspoon rosemary
1 teaspoon basil
1 teaspoon thyme
1 bay leaf
32 fl oz (900 ml) velouté (see page 8) made with chicken stock, water or half of each
seasoning
chopped parsley for garnish — optional

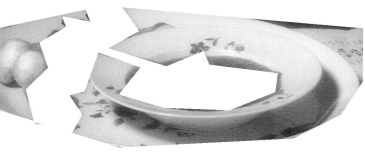

Melt the butter in a large saucepan. Add the mushrooms, onions, garlic, herbs and the bay leaf.

Sauté the mixture for 10 minutes, stirring occasionally.

While the mushroom mixture is cooking make the velouté with the stock or water (see page 8).

Strain the prepared velouté onto the mushrooms and simmer slowly for 15 minutes.

Season to taste and serve with chopped parsley sprinkled over the soup.

Serving suggestions:

☆ 2 - 3 fl oz (50 - 90 ml) cream can be stirred into the soup for a more luxurious texture. Add the cream during the final 10 minutes of cooking and allow to simmer gently.

☆ Swirl a tablespoon of double cream or crème fraîche onto each soup bowl just before it goes to the table.

☆ Light, crunchy garlic croûtons would be a nice addition to this soup, (see page 4) — you may wish to reduce the amount of garlic in the soup to allow for the garlic croûtons.

Chef's tips:

☆ A few fresh or dried (and soaked) wild mushrooms certainly wouldn't hurt this soup. If you use dried mushrooms, let them soak in slightly warm water for a good hour before using, and then reserve the flavoured water to use for the velouté.

☆ Dried mushrooms are available from good delicatessens. Assorted fresh mushrooms are available in season from upmarket supermarkets and vegetable suppliers.

Wine:
☆ Quite a big red would work well: Spanish Rioja or an oaky Chilean Cabernet Sauvignon.

CHINESE CHICKEN, MUSHROOM, EGGDROP SOUP

Serves: 4
Preparation time: 15 minutes
Cooking time: 15 minutes
Suitable for dinner party: Yes
Suitable first course: Yes
Suitable microwave cooking: Reheating only
Suitable freezing: Yes (omit sesame oil if freezing — add prior to serving)
Special equipment: None
Calorie content: Medium
Carbohydrate content: Medium-low
Fibre content: Low
Protein content: Medium
Fat content: Medium-low

This is a very innovative and exciting soup, with many versatile finishes. Once you have assembled the ingredients it is surprisingly quick and simple to make, and the complexity of flavours will impress your guests no end!

 26

1 tablespoon peanut or vegetable oil
28 fl oz (800 ml) chicken stock
8 oz (225 gm) chicken breast, skinless, boneless, in small dice
8 oz (225 gm) mushrooms, sliced
3 cloves of garlic, peeled and crushed
2½ oz (65 gm) spring onion, chopped quite fine
1 egg, lightly beaten
4 - 8 tablespoons Chinese oyster sauce*
Few drops toasted sesame oil for garnish*

A wok is the most practical cooking vessel for this soup — if you don't own one, a large, heavy saucepan would be fine.

Have all the prepared ingredients close at hand when you begin this soup. Things happen very quickly, once started.

Preheat a dry wok over a high heat for 2 - 3 minutes.

Add the oil and immediately add the mushrooms, chicken and garlic. Stir constantly over high heat for 5 minutes. (Your kitchen will look and smell as fragrant and smoky as a Chinese restaurant kitchen at this point).

Add the chicken stock and bring to the boil.

Trickle the beaten egg into the centre of the soup whilst whisking briskly with a small whisk or fork. The egg will set into fine shreds.

Once the egg is incorporated turn the heat down to simmer.

Add the spring onion and oyster sauce and simmer for 5 minutes.

 27

Serve in deep bowls (Chinese if you have them!) and sprinkle 2 - 3 drops of sesame oil on each soup just prior to serving.

☆   ☆   ☆

Serving suggestions:
☆ The chicken breast can be omitted totally or replaced by making tiny dumplings of ground chicken, sesame seeds and a few drops of sesame oil. Poach the dumplings for the final 5 - 8 minutes of cooking — omit the sesame oil garnish.
☆ *Or* add shreds of leftover roast meat during final 5 minutes of cooking.

☆ *Or* make Won-ton* purses filled with left-over cooked meat (chopped fine or ground) mixed with onion and seasoning and poach for the final 5 minutes of cooking.

Chef's tip:
☆ No additional seasoning is necessary as the oyster sauce is quite salty. Oyster sauce varies greatly in strength. Taste the soup after 4 table-spoons have been added; then add more according to taste.

Wine:
☆ I would enjoy a spicy Gewurztraminer from Alsace or a fruity Rosé with this multi-dimensional soup.

* If you are fortunate enough to have a Chinese store in your area you will find all the above ingredients there. If not you will find everything but the Won-ton wrappers at any up-market supermarket or delicatessen.

 29

SALMON CHOWDER

Serves: 4
Preparation time: 15 minutes
Cooking time: 25 minutes
Suitable for dinner party: Yes
Suitable first course: Yes
Suitable microwave cooking: No
Suitable freezing: No
Special equipment: None
Calorie content: Medium-high
Carbohydrate content: Low
Fibre content: Low
Protein content: High
Fat content: Medium-high

A sophisticated and delicious meal in a bowl
which would make a rather special lunch treat
or light supper.

 30

2 oz (50 gm) butter
1 lb (450 gm) salmon, skin and bones removed, cut into ¾ inch cubes
1 lb (450 gm) smoked bacon, rindless, diced small (optional)
2 sticks celery in small dice
1 courgette in small dice
1 small onion, peeled and diced
30 fl oz (850 ml) of fish velouté (see page 6)
1 bay leaf
4 teaspoons fresh dill
1 clove garlic, peeled and chopped finely
2 small red (sweet) peppers in small dice
1 tablespoon tomato paste
seasoning

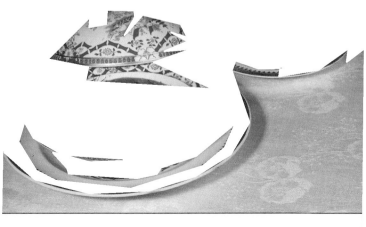

In a heavy soup pot melt the butter over medium heat.

Add the bacon, celery, sweet pepper, onion and garlic and sauté, stirring for 10 minutes without browning.

Stir in the tomato paste and cook for a further minute.

Pour in the fish velouté, the dill and the bay leaf and slowly bring to the boil. Let the soup simmer for 10 minutes.

Add the salmon cubes and stir carefully to prevent them from sticking to the pan. The salmon takes no more than 5 minutes to cook!

Season with sea salt and freshly-ground black pepper and serve immediately.

Serving suggestions:
☆ To make this a more substantial soup — suitable for a light one-course meal — add 2 medium-sized potatoes, peeled and diced small, with the first ingredients.

Chef's tip:
☆ If making fish stock with this soup in mind you might want to tailor your stock to the soup by using salmon bones.

Wine:
☆ This soup deserves a fine white Burgundy if your budget allows. Alternatively go for any well made Chardonnay, dryish Riesling, young, fruity red or white Rully from the Côte Chalonaise or New Zealand Pinot Noir.

LEEK AND POTATO SOUP WITH SWEETCORN

Serves: 4
Preparation time: 15 minutes
Cooking time: 25 minutes
Suitable for dinner party: Yes
Suitable first course: Yes
Suitable microwave cooking: Reheating only
Suitable freezing: Yes
Special equipment: Electric hand blender or food processor
Calorie content: Quite low
Carbohydrate content: High
Fibre content: High
Protein content: Medium-low
Fat content: Medium-low (very low if using low-fat milk)

Silky and luxuriously-textured leek and potato soup has always been a treat and with the added bonus of being incredibly inexpensive. A fun twist on this classic theme is the addition of buttery and light, crunchy corn kernels.

 33

1½ lbs (700 gm) leeks, washed, coarsely chopped
1½ lbs (700 gm) potatoes, peeled and sliced
1 onion, peeled and coarsely chopped
8 oz (225 gm) sweetcorn, fresh or canned
¼ cup olive oil
32 fl oz (900 ml) water or chicken stock
2 bay leaves
2 teaspoons thyme
1½ cups milk, whole or low fat
seasoning

In a large saucepan warm the olive oil and add the potatoes, leek, onion and thyme. Sauté over medium heat for 10 minutes, stirring often.

Add the water and bay leaves and bring to the boil. Reduce the heat and simmer for 25 minutes.

Remove from the heat, fish out the bay leaves and coarsely mash or purée the soup (depending on the desired texture) in the pot.

Pour in the milk and bring back to a gentle simmer, whilst stirring continually.

If the soup is very thick at this stage, add a little more milk or water.

Add the corn kernels and season with salt and pepper. Cook the soup for 2 more minutes, stirring, and serve.

☆　☆　☆

Serving suggestions:
☆ Sprinkle with chopped parsley and serve

with plenty of whole-grain bread for a healthy and delightful meal.

☆ An interesting variation is the addition of a few rashers of smoked bacon — cut into very small pieces — with the potatoes and leeks.

Chef's tip:
☆ If freezing this soup, omit the corn until the final reheating before serving. Of course, if you wish, the corn can be omitted from the recipe totally.

Wine:
☆ A rich, buttery Chardonnay would comple- ment this soup well. Look to Australia, California or perhaps one of the new breeds of super Vins de Pays from the South of France.

MUSHROOM, BACON AND RED PEPPER PURÉE

Serves: 4
Preparation time: 12 minutes
Cooking time: 40 minutes
Suitable for dinner party: Yes
Suitable first course: Yes
Suitable microwave cooking: Reheating only
Suitable freezing: Yes
Special equipment: Electric hand blender or food
    processor
Calorie content: Medium
Carbohydrate content: Medium
Fibre content: Medium
Protein content: Medium-high
Fat content: Medium-high

This is a vibrantly-flavoured puréed soup that makes a tasty and satisfying light meal or a punchy introduction to dinner.

 36

1 lb (450 gm) mushrooms, sliced
12 oz (350 gm) bacon, rindless and chopped
2 sweet red peppers, coarsely cut
1 medium onion, coarsely chopped
2 cloves of garlic, peeled and crushed
6 oz (175 gm) potato, peeled and coarsely cut
32 fl oz (900 ml) chicken stock
1½ oz (37.5 gm) butter
1 teaspoon tarragon
1 teaspoon thyme
1 teaspoon basil
pinch of rosemary
seasoning
2 fl oz (50 ml) double cream

In a large saucepan melt the butter and gently sauté the onions, mushrooms, peppers, potato, garlic and bacon for 7 minutes, stirring occasionally.

When the vegetables are soft, add the herbs and stir for 1 minute.

Add the stock and bring to the boil. Lower the heat and simmer for 20 minutes.

Remove the pot from the heat and purée the soup. Bring back to a light boil. (If you plan to add cream, this is the time to stir it in. Allow it to simmer for 1 minute). Season with salt and pepper and serve.

Chef's tip:
☆ If you are not using cream and find the soup

too thick, add a little milk or water to produce the desired consistency.

Wine:
☆ Big, clean, fruit flavours would be best with this soup, for instance, a racy Sauvignon Blanc from New Zealand or a young, zippy Californian Zinfandel, perhaps.

COLD CHERRY SOUP

Serves: 4
Type of dish: Dessert or snack
Preparation time: 15 minutes
Cooking time: 8 minutes
Waiting time: 15 minutes
Suitable for dinner party: Yes
Suitable first course: No
Suitable microwave cooking: No
Suitable freezing: Yes
Special equipment: None
Calorie content: Low
Carbohydrate content: High
Fibre content: High
Protein content: Low
Fat content: Low

People seem startled at the concept of a fruit
soup yet they are a part of the everyday diet in
some countries. In Sweden, for example,
blueberry or rosehip soup would be a typical,
nutritious and delicious treat for children after
school. This is a more adult version, suitable
for dessert, but it can easily be adapted for
your children by omitting the wine.

 39

1½ lbs (700 gm) fresh cherries, stones removed & reserved
25 fl oz (725 ml) water
2 oz (50 gm) sugar
juice of 2 lemons
grated rind of 1 lemon
1 cinnamon stick
12 fl oz (350 ml) sweet white wine
4 tablespoons crème fraîche, double cream or plain yoghurt

Put the cherry stalks, stones, cinnamon stick, white wine, (and any cherry juice) plus the water into a heavy saucepan.

Bring to the boil and simmer gently for 5 minutes.

Turn off the heat and let the liquid rest, covered, for 15 minutes.

Strain the liquid and bring back to the boil. Add the cherries and the lemon juice and simmer for 1 minute.

Remove from the heat and cool. Refrigerate until ready to serve.

☆   ☆   ☆

Serving suggestions:
☆ Swirl a tablespoon of cream or yoghurt onto each bowl and, if you have one, garnish with a mint leaf.

Chef's tip:
☆ Fruit soup can be made with most berries

that are ripe and flavourful. Try blueberry or strawberry and replace the 2 fl oz (50 ml) of wine with 1 - 2 fl oz (25 - 50 ml) of any orange-based liqueur, and one of the lemons with an orange.

Wine:
☆ Try a chilled glass of Coteaux du Layon, or similar sweet wine, from the Loire.

YELLOW PEA, CARROT AND HAM SOUP

Serves: 4
Preparation time: 5 minutes
Cooking time: 2 hours
Suitable for dinner party: Rustic style
Suitable first course: Yes
Suitable microwave cooking: Reheating only
Suitable freezing: Yes
Special equipment: No
Calorie content: Low
Carbohydrate content: High
Fibre content: High
Protein content: Low
Fat content: Low

1 lb (450 gm) split yellow peas	
4 oz (125 gm) smoked ham, julienned	
1 medium onion, peeled and halved	
3 medium carrots, peeled and whole	
4 garlic cloves, peeled and whole	
4 cloves	
3 bay leaves	
water or chicken stock	
seasoning	

Rinse the peas and then soak them overnight in a large container with plenty of fresh water (allow a few inches of extra water as the peas will swell up).

Discard the soaking water and rinse the peas well. Transfer them to a soup pot and add water or chicken stock to cover the peas plus 1 inch.

Use the cloves to pin the bay leaves to the onion halves and add them to the pot along with the garlic and the whole carrots.

Cook over medium-low heat, stirring every few minutes. Then simmer gently for one and a half hours. Remove any scum as it appears and add more water if the soup becomes too thick.

Remove the carrots and cut into small dice then return them to the pot.

Discard the onion, bay leaf and cloves.

When the peas are thoroughly cooked and a pulp-like consistency has been reached, season the soup to taste and serve with an ounce of ham strewn over each bowl.

Serving suggestions:
☆ This soup is just delicious with baked garlic bread.

Chef's tip:
☆ When reheating this soup you will need to add a little water or stock and stir well as you bring the soup to the boil.

Wine:
☆ A light, young Spanish red would complement this earthy potage.

CURRIED MUSSEL SOUP WITH VEGETABLES

Serves: 4
Preparation time: 20 minutes
Cooking time: 25 minutes
Suitable for dinner party: Yes
Suitable first course: Yes
Suitable microwave cooking: No
Suitable freezing: No
Special equipment: Fine sieve
Calorie content: Quite low
Carbohydrate content: Quite low
Fibre content: Quite low
Protein content: High
Fat content: Medium-low

 45

3 lbs (1.3 kg) fresh live mussels, cleaned*
1 carrot - peeled and diced small
1 medium courgette, diced small
1 small onion, peeled and diced small
1 celery stock, diced small
1 sweet, red pepper, diced small
1 green pepper, diced small
26 fl oz (750 ml) fish velouté
3 oz (75 gm) butter
2 cloves garlic, chopped finely
1 cup dry white wine
4 sprigs chopped parsley
2½ teaspoons mild curry powder
pinch of thyme
2 fl oz (50 ml) double cream

In a saucepan (with a lid) melt half the butter and sauté the onions for 3 minutes without browning. Add the white wine, garlic, 1 cup of the water and the mussels. Stir well and put the lid on. Cook for 3 minutes over medium heat, stir well, replace the lid and cook for a further 2 minutes. Repeat until most of the mussels have opened.*

Once they have cooled, remove the mussels with a slotted spoon and lay them out on a flat tray to cool. Reserve the mussel stock you have just made.

Remove the mussels from their shells. Refrigerate them, covered, until later. Add any liquid on the tray to the mussel stock.

In a large saucepan sauté all the diced vegetables in the remaining butter for 5 minutes, stirring often.

Strain the mussel stock, through a very fine sieve or doubled cheesecloth (to remove any sand or grit), onto the vegetables.

Add the 26 fl oz (750 ml) of velouté. Add the curry powder and thyme and simmer for 15 minutes.

Stir in the cream and the mussels, check the seasoning and simmer for 2 minutes more.

Stir in chopped parsley (or chives) and serve.

Chef's tip:
☆ *Any mussels that remain closed after cooking MUST be discarded. Do not force any mussels open. To test whether a mussel is good before cooking — tap any open mussel

against a hard surface as you clean it. If it does not close it is dead and should be discarded!

Wine:
☆ A dry, crisp white is called for here. Virtually any dry Loire white would suit. Other options: Pinot Grigio from Northern Italy or a somewhat fuller white Crozes-Hermitage.

BANG BANG CHICKEN SOUP

Serves: 4
Preparation time: 15 minutes
Cooking time: 40 minutes
Suitable for dinner party: Yes
Suitable first course: Yes
Suitable microwave cooking: Reheating liquid
    part only
Suitable freezing: Yes — liquid part only
Special equipment: Sieve
Calorie content: High
Carbohydrate content: Medium
Fibre content: High
Protein content: High
Fat content: High

This is a wonderful East-West crossover soup
based on the Chinese dish of the same name. It
is a spicy peanut soup garnished with cold strips
of chicken breast and cucumber.

 49

8 oz (225 gm) chicken breast (boneless & skinned)
8 oz (225 gm) peanut butter — smooth or crunchy
6 oz (175 gm) unsalted peanuts
2 tablespoons butter
2 sweet, red peppers, coarsely chopped
1 medium onion, coarsely chopped
3 teaspoon Szechuan peppercorns*
32 fl oz (900 ml) water
2 - 4 tablespoons Chinese Satay sauce*
Cucumber julienne for garnish

Poach or steam the chicken breast until cooked through — approximately 10 minutes. Cool and cut into julienne. Cover and refrigerate.

Julienne the cucumber for later — allow 1 heaped tablespoon per person.

Sauté the peppers, onions, peppercorns and peanuts in the butter, without browning, for 10 minutes.

Make a stock by adding the water and simmering for 20 minutes.

Strain the stock and purée the solids with a small amount of the liquid.

Pass the purée through a sieve, back into the stock, pressing on the solids to capture all the liquid. Discard the solids.

Return the stock to the stove and add the Satay sauce and peanut butter and simmer gently for 10 minutes. Check seasoning.

Ladle the soup into the bowls — three-quarters full only — and pile a mound of cold chicken and cucumber strips in the centre of the bowls.

Chef's tips:
☆ *Satay sauce and Szechuan peppercorns can be found in Chinese stores or larger supermarkets.

Satay sauce varies from brand to brand, some can be quite hot. If in doubt try 2 tablespoons, simmer for a few minutes and check the flavour before adding more.

Wine:
☆ It is difficult to match a wine with hot or

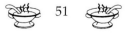

spicy foods but you might try an equally spicy
Alsace Gewurztraminer or a clean, refreshing,
New World Sauvignon Blanc.

CHEESE AND ALE SOUP

Serves: 4
Preparation time: 15 minutes
Cooking time: 35 minutes
Suitable for dinner party: Yes
Suitable first course: Yes
Suitable microwave cooking: Reheating only
Suitable freezing: Yes
Special equipment: None
Calorie content: Quite high
Carbohydrate content: Quite low
Fibre content: Low
Protein content: High
Fat content: Quite high

12 oz (350 gm) strong Cheddar cheese, grated
1 can (14 fl oz) Bitter ale
½ small onion, diced
1½ oz (37.5 gm) butter
32 fl oz (900 ml) chicken velouté (see page 8)
2 cloves garlic, crushed
3 tablespoons spring onions, chopped
1 teaspoon thyme
1 teaspoon basil
2 fl oz (50 ml) cream, optional

In a large saucepan melt the butter and sweat the onions with the garlic, thyme and basil for about 5 minutes.

Add the ale and bring to the boil. Simmer uncovered for 7 minutes. The liquid will reduce slightly.

Add the chicken velouté and bring to the boil. Then turn down the heat until the liquid is just simmering.

Stir in the grated cheese and spring onions. Simmer for 20 minutes.

Add cream if you wish and then check seasoning. Add salt and fresh ground pepper as required and serve.

Serving suggestions:
☆ Make crunchy, golden croûtons by dicing day-old bread and sautéeing in a little butter until golden. Transfer to absorbent paper and add to soup when served.

Chef's tip:
☆ This recipe makes a light, rather refined style of soup, ideal for dinner parties or lunch. If you would like a more robustly flavoured soup — increase the amount of cheese by 4 oz (125 gm) and use 1 whole onion.

Once the cheese is added, stir often, as the cheese may fall to the bottom and burn.

Wine:
☆ Actually a glass of beer would be ideal, but a warm, rustic, red wine, for instance from the Languedoc or Provence, would also be a suitable partner.

TOMATO SOUP

Serves: 4
Preparation time: 15 minutes
Cooking time: 30 minutes
Suitable for dinner party: Yes
Suitable first course: Yes
Suitable microwave cooking: Reheating only
Suitable freezing: Yes
Special equipment: Hand blender or food processor
Calorie content: Low
Carbohydrate content: Medium-high
Fibre content: Medium
Protein content: Medium
Fat content: Low

A fresh-tasting, simple soup that can be made into a sophisticated dinner party dish with the addition of a tasty topping.

 56

3 lbs (1.3 kgs) ripe tomatoes, quartered
1 onion, peeled and sliced
2 celery sticks, chopped coarsely
2 tablespoons tomato paste
32 fl oz (900ml) chicken stock (or water)
1 tablespoon vegetable oil
1 tablespoon butter
1 teaspoon each thyme, basil and tarragon

In a large soup pot sauté the tomatoes, onions, thyme, tarragon and celery in the oil and butter, without browning, for 7 minutes.

Stir in the tomato paste and cook a further 3

 57

minutes, stirring continually.

Add the stock (or water) and simmer for 15 minutes.

Remove from the heat and blend the soup, with a hand blender, then pass the liquid through a sieve and back to the pot, (or transfer to a food processor to blend and then sieve the soup back into the pot), pressing down on any solids to extract all the flavour.

Bring the soup back to a boil, add the basil and simmer for a couple of minutes. Season to taste and serve.

Serving suggestions:
☆ The simplicity of this soup makes it very versatile — enjoy it as lunch with fresh, crusty bread, as a first course with crunchy, cheese croûtons (see page 3) or a swirl of crème fraîche and a few torn Basil leaves. Or even dress it up for a dinner party with a topping of spinach-cream cheese croûtons.

SPINACH-CREAM CHEESE CROÛTONS

2 large slices bread
1 tablespoon butter
2 oz (50 gm) cream cheese
Few leaves spinach
Pinch nutmeg
seasoning

Blanche the leaves for 2 mins in boiling water then cool, squeeze out all the water and finely

 58

chop and season with salt, pepper and nutmeg.

Cut out four 2-inch discs from the bread and sauté gently in the butter until golden on both sides.

Spread the cheese on the discs and pile the spinach mixture on the top.

Float one croûton on each bowl of soup.

Chef's tip:
☆ Any really ripe tomatoes are suitable for this soup.

Wine:
☆ It is difficult to suggest a wine with tomatoes due to their high acidity. By all means try an inexpensive Mediterranean red and save your fine wine for another occasion.

ONION SOUP

Serves: 4
Preparation time: 10 minutes
Cooking time: 40 minutes
Suitable for dinner party: Yes
Suitable first course: Yes
Suitable microwave cooking: Reheating only —
    grill croûtons separately
Suitable freezing: Yes (without the topping)
Special equipment: None
Calorie content: Medium
Carbohydrate content: Medium-high
Fibre content: Medium
Protein content: Medium
Fat content: Medium

3 medium onions, peeled, sliced thinly	
3 cloves garlic, crushed	
35 fl oz (950 ml) chicken stock	
2 tablespoons flour	
8 fl oz (225 ml) red wine	
1 teaspoon tarragon	
1 teaspoon basil	
1 teaspoon thyme	
1 teaspoon oregano	
2 bay leaves	
1½ oz (37.5 gm) butter	

 61

Melt the butter in a large saucepan. Sauté the onions over quite high heat, stirring often, for 15 minutes. Brown the onions well, stirring constantly the last few minutes.

When the onions are very brown, add the flour and stir for 1 minute.

Stir in the wine, bring to a simmer and reduce for 2 minutes.

Add the stock, herbs and bay leaf and bring to the boil, reduce the heat slightly and simmer for 15 minutes.

Season and serve into ovenproof soup bowls, top each with a cheese croûton (see below) and bake in a hot oven (or under the grill) until the cheese is melted and bubbling and serve.

Serving suggestions:
☆ Sprinkle with chopped parsley or chives for colour.
☆ Serve with plenty of fresh, crusty bread.

Chef's tip:
☆ The chicken stock can be replaced by water (although with some loss of flavour and body), or with half stock and half water.

CHEESE CROÛTONS

4 slices of bread
2 - 3 oz (50 - 75 gm) Gruyère or medium Cheddar, grated
olive oil

Cut the bread into approximately 2½ inch circles and brush them lightly, both sides, with the oil. Bake.in a hot oven until golden and reserve until needed. (The croûtons will keep for a couple of days in an airtight container.)

Place the croûtons on the soups, top them with grated cheese and bake them.

Wine:
☆ A robust country red from the Mediterranean, Côtes-du-Rhône or perhaps an Australian Shiraz.

THAI STYLE CHICKEN AND COCONUT SOUP

Serves: 4
Preparation time: 15 minutes
Cooking time: 20 minutes
Suitable for dinner party: Yes
Suitable first course: Yes
Suitable microwave cooking: No
Suitable freezing: Yes
Special equipment: None
Calorie content: Low
Carbohydrate content: Medium
Fibre content: Low
Protein content: Medium
Fat content: Low

This is a marvellous and authentically-flavoured
Thai soup. You can vary the amount of spices and
heat according to your taste. The following is well
flavoured with a bit of a kick but not too hot for
those who are not used to Asian flavours.

 64

8 oz (225 gm) skinless chicken breast
2 garlic cloves, crushed
3 tablespoons vegetable oil
2 tablespoons mild curry powder*
one 4 inch piece lemongrass, minced*
½ oz (12.5 gm) fresh ginger, minced
16 fl oz (450 ml) chicken stock
16 fl oz (450 ml) coconut milk *
6 fl oz (175 ml) water
1 small hot chili pepper, seeded and chopped fine
4 oz (125 gm) fine rice noodles *
juice of 1 lime
6 tablespoons Thai fish sauce*
coriander for garnish, optional

Soak the noodles in warm water for a few minutes then cook them in a pot of boiling water for 4 minutes. Drain and refresh the noodles under cold running water. Cut the chicken breast into ½ inch crossways strips.

In a large wok or pot sauté the garlic in the oil, over low heat, until it softens, about 4 minutes. Stir in the curry powder and continue stirring over heat until it is incorporated into the oil. Add the lemongrass, ginger, chili, water, stock and coconut milk and bring to a boil. Add the chicken strips and simmer for 8 minutes. Add the lime and fish sauce to taste.

Divide the noodles between 4 deep prewarmed bowls and pour the soup over the noodles. Sprinkle fresh chopped coriander over the top and serve.

Serving suggestions:
☆ This soup looks really good served in deep Chinese-style bowls with Chinese spoons.

Chef's tips:
☆ Always wear rubber gloves when preparing fresh chilis and be sure to avoid touching your eyes or mouth if you have handled the peppers. If you do so accidentally wash the affected area with plenty of cold water.

Wine:
☆ A cold Thai beer would be suitable with this soup.

* Ingredients available in most good supermarkets or Asian stores.

GASPACHO

Serves: 4
Preparation time: 15 minutes
Preparation start time: 6 - 24 hours before serving
Suitable for dinner party: Yes
Suitable for first course: Yes
Suitable for microwave cooking: No
Suitable for freezing: No
Special equipment: Blender, food processor or pestle & mortar
Calorie content: Low
Carbohydrate content: High
Fibre content: High
Protein content: Low
Fat content: Low

A wonderful, cooling, rustic soup from Spain. There are many regional variations, and no hard and fast rules, so feel free to experiment with the ingredients and the seasoning.

8 oz (225 gm) ripe tomatoes
4 oz (125 gm) cucumber, peeled
1 small red pepper, seeds removed
1 small green (sweet) pepper, seeds removed
1 small onion, peeled
1 - 2 garlic cloves, peeled
2 tablespoons (30 gm) soft breadcrumbs
4 fl oz (125 ml) tomato juice
1 fl oz (25 ml) olive oil
4 fresh basil leaves or 1 teaspoon oregano
seasoning
fresh lime or lemon juice to taste.

Blanch the tomatoes for a few seconds, leave to cool for 1 minute, then slip off the skins.

Chop all the vegetables, including the garlic, finely.

Using a food processor or pestle and mortar blend a quarter of the vegetables with the garlic and breadcrumbs until smooth, adding some of the tomato juice as you blend.

Transfer to a serving tureen and stir in the remaining liquids and the chopped vegetables. Season to taste with sea salt and fresh black pepper.

Chill for several hours or overnight to allow the flavours to develop.

Just prior to serving tear the basil and add it (or the oregano) and check the seasoning. Serve very cold with added ice cubes if desired.

Chef's tip:
☆ Add a few drops of Worcestershire or Tabasco sauce for a spicy Gaspacho.
☆ We use a mixture of tomato juice and chicken stock for a fuller-flavoured soup.

Wine:
☆ Drink a chilled glass of Fino sherry with this summer soup.

70